Billiards for Everyone

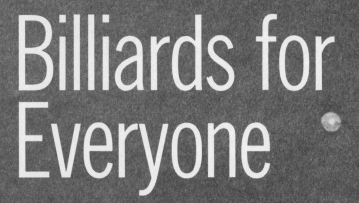

Billiards for Everyone

By Luther Lassiter
World Pocket Billiard Champion

with George Sullivan

GROSSET & DUNLAP
A NATIONAL GENERAL COMPANY
Publishers · New York

1973 Printing

COPYRIGHT © 1965 FLEET PUBLISHING CORP.
PHOTOS ON PAGES 43, 65, 67 & HISTORY PAGE 7 APPEARED
ORIGINALLY IN THE MODERN GUIDE TO POCKET BILLIARDS
ISBN: 0-448-01519-6
PUBLISHED SIMULTANEOUSLY IN CANADA
LIBRARY OF CONGRESS CATALOG CARD NUMBER: 65-18455

For help in preparation of this book, grateful acknowledgment is made to photographer Barrett Gallagher who shot the extraordinary continuous-sequence action pictures; photographer Phil Bath; Ted Eliades of Ransom Billiards; and Stanley G. Markusen, Executive Director, Billiard Room Proprietors Association of America.

BOOK DESIGN: TERRY MONTALVO
PRINTED IN THE UNITED STATES OF AMERICA

CONTENTS

BILLIARDS' PAST

The game of pocket billiards, known in every corner of the country as pool, developed into its present form in the 1800's and, discounting its present resurgence, reached a height of popularity in the late 1920's and early 1930's.

The precise origin of the game is obscure, though historians trace the present-day variation to 14th-century England where it was derived from the popular pastime of lawn bowling or "bowles." First it was brought in out of the cold fog of the British Isles, then it was played with a clublike stick to compensate for the reduced playing area indoors. Another rule change called for the ball to be pushed instead of rapped. And finally someone suggested the whole affair be transferred to a tabletop; the game of billiards was born.

At first the table had only two pockets. Then two more were added and later the table itself was converted to its present oblong shape with the addition of still two more pockets.

Billiards made its entry into the United States in 1565. As time went on players of skill introduced refinements to the game. In 1878 the first professional championship matches were held. Participants dressed in black tie, a custom maintained to this day which identifies billiards as "the aristocrat of sports."

In recent years, both as sport and business enterprise, billiards has made great strides. No longer is the game played in dingy basement pool halls by the more unsavory members of the community. Big, bright, modern, air-conditioned billiard palaces have sprung up in almost every American city. Even the word "pool," identified with the game's lesser status two decades ago, is passing out of favor. Today almost everywhere the sport is called "billiards."

TAKE YOUR CUE FROM ME

Two words sum up my credo for playing billiards at your best: BE NATURAL.

In the photographs in this book I show you stance and stroke and strategy that will guide you as you acquire skill. Don't try to imitate too closely what you see here. Let your playing acquire its own style. As you stand at the table, as you grip the cue, as you stroke, be relaxed and comfortable.

No one, not even a championship player, should ever say to you, "This is the way you must do it." There are few "musts" in pocket billiards. To a great extent it's going to be up to you to develop the technique that will bring you the greatest success.

Billiards looks easy when you're watching an expert—but don't be fooled! It is an easy game to learn, given accurate instruction such as you will find in these pages. But becoming really good at the game takes long, constant, daily practice to perfect those reflexes, to measure distances and angles dead accurately by eye.

That's the never ending challenge of billiards. It will always be fun as many years as you care to go on playing—and improving.

So chalk up your cue and let me show you how to begin.

LUTHER LASSITER

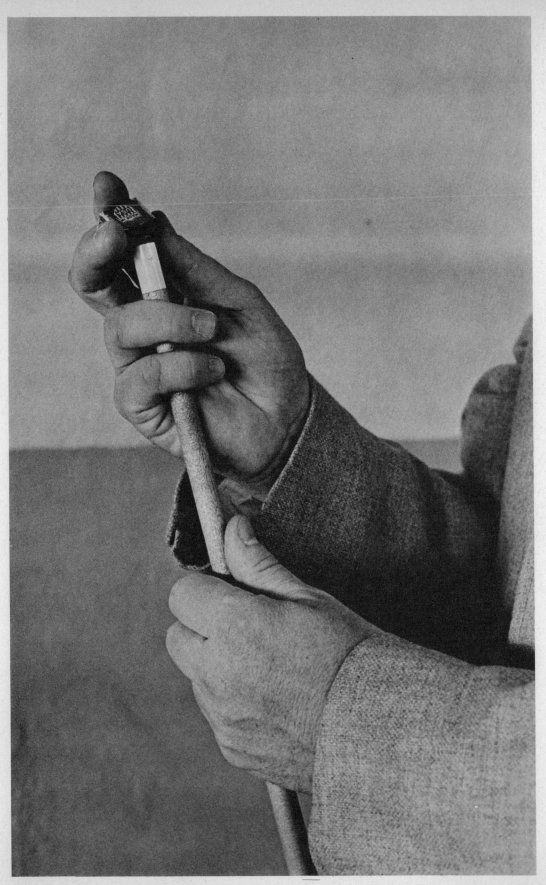

So that the cue won't slip off the cue ball when I stroke, I brush chalk on the cue tip. I do this before every shot.

HOW TO HOLD THE CUE

The most important thing to know about the grip is that it should be purely a finger grip; the palm of the hand should never come in contact with the cue.

Double up your *fingers*; notice the channel they form. To grip properly, simply let the cue rest in this channel. The thumb circles around the cue, but it merely guides; it never squeezes.

Some players grip the cue by using a channel formed by the three middle fingers plus the thumb. The little finger arches above the stick. If this style feels comfortable to you, use it. As the photos to the right indicate, the author favors a grip using all four fingers.

Where do you grip the cue? Just about every professional player will tell you to take your grip at the stick's balancing point or an inch or two or three in back of this point. A faulty stroke is almost sure to result if your grip is positioned forward of the balancing or too far back toward the butt end of the cue.

Once you've found a grip that satisfies you, stick with it. Use the same type of finger hold and the same amount of finger pressure with every shot.

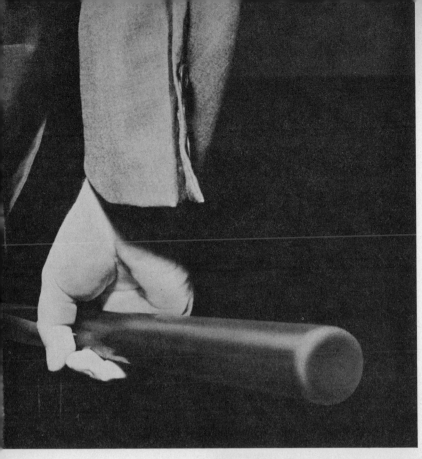

I use a four-finger grip, but some players are successful using three. Notice how my fingers merely cradle the cue, and how the palm of my hand does not come in contact with the stick at all.

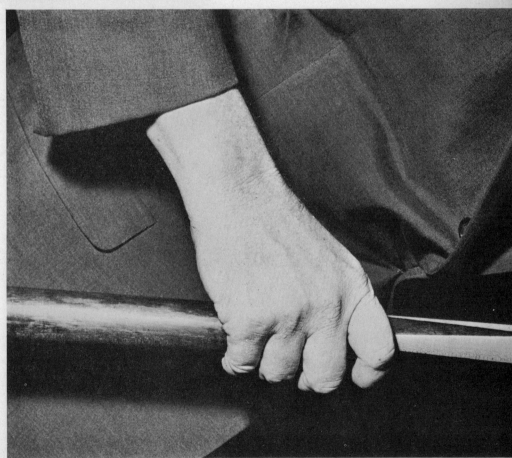

How to Make the Finger Bridge

Developing a proper finger bridge—the rest and guide for your cue—is a simple matter.

First, bring the tips of your thumb and index finger together so they form a flattened circle. Then extend and spread apart the other three fingers.

Next, place the *heel* of the hand and the extended fingers on the table, keeping in mind that most of the weight should be concentrated on the heel of the hand.

Finally, place the cue between the thumb and index finger, laying the stick on the thumb at the point where the thumb joins the hand. Stroke the cue. If the stroke lacks control, tighten up the forefinger. In other words, decrease the size of the flattened circle. If, on the other hand, you are finding it difficult to get a smooth stroke, loosen up the forefinger grip.

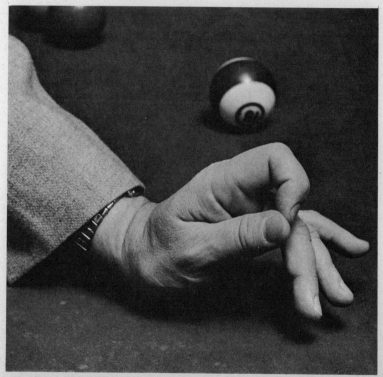

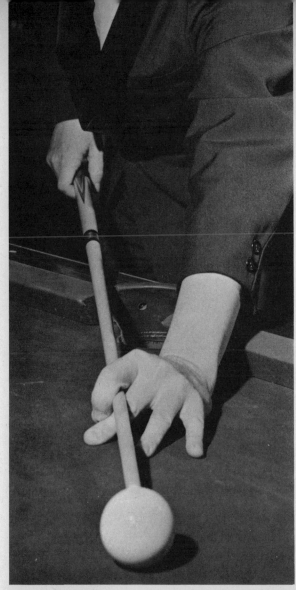

Since it guides and even steers the cue, the bridge is all-important. On every stroke you have to be certain that your bridge is going to provide solid and wavering support for your stick.

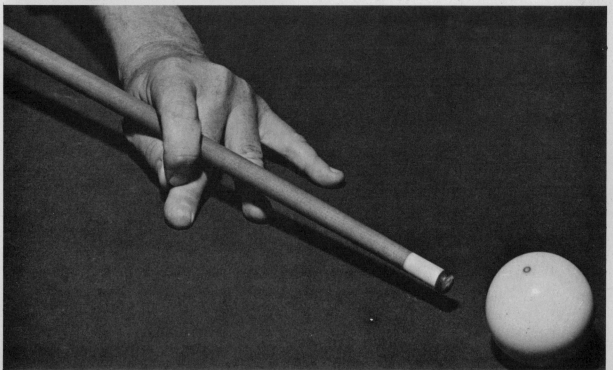

Position and balance are what are important in the stance. On any conventional shot, position yourself 10 to 12 inches from the table. Face the direction of the shot, your right hand and arm lined up with the cue ball. Now draw the right foot back, so it is almost behind the left, about 18 inches from it. Angle the left foot toward the shot.

Bend forward from the waist, extending your left arm, and place the left hand in its bridge position six to eight inches from the cue ball.

Your right arm should be completely free to swing the cue to and fro.

Your head should be positioned directly over the cue, for you must be able to sight down it as a marksman sights down a gun barrel.

Depending upon the position of the cue ball, you may have to move nearer to or farther away from the table. But no matter where you take your stance, or what variations you employ, it is always a cardinal rule to have your head positioned directly over the cue.

A cardinal rule of billiards: your head must always be positioned directly over the cue.

The left arm should be extended; the left hand should be positioned six to eight inches from the cue ball.

One element characterizes the play of every professional billiard player I have ever seen. Each has a stroke that is smooth and springy from start to finish.

Of course, the billiard stroke is really a two-phase action. There is a backswing, then a forward swing. These two actions must be blended together into a single rhythmic motion. I always compare the billiard stroke to the arm motion a woman uses when she is ironing clothes. It must be smooth, almost without any effort at all.

Throughout the stroke, you must remember to hold your cue almost perfectly level. I realize that sometimes this isn't possible, as for instance when you are attempting to shoot over obstructing balls, but generally speaking, try to keep the cue parallel to the table.

Before you strike the ball, take a few practice strokes. Stroke the cue back and forth, stopping it just before it touches the cue ball. This action is comparable to the golfer's "waggle" before he swings. And like the waggle, your practice stroke will set the rhythm for your shot.

THE SECRET OF
THE STROKE

*In the Victorian era
billiards was played under gaslight.*

The Backswing

When you've lined up the shot (*as at left*), the drawing back of the cue (*facing page*) is called the backswing. Beware of tension in the backswing. As you draw it back, be careful not to tighten up your grip on the cue. Continue merely cradling it in your right hand.

Keep your wrist tension free, too, for when you come through with the stroke, you must snap your wrist if you want to give power and authority to your shot. You won't be able to do this if your wrist is tightened up.

Your right arm should be kept close to your body as you bring the cue back.

Try to visualize the entire stroke as being like a pendulum on a grandfather's clock; it is smooth and easy and follows a precise path, back and forward.

The Forward Swing

Without changing the pressure of the grip, bring the cue straight forward, and continue the stroke until the cue reaches a point three or four inches beyond where the cue ball rested before it was hit. In other words, stroke as if you were actually shooting through the cue ball, as demonstrated in the continuous-sequence picture on this page.

This follow-through motion is an important element in every single stroke. And remember when you follow-through, don't let the cue tip waver to the right or left; keep the entire stick on the track.

Remember: the stroke moves backward, forward, and follows through in one single fluid action.

My eyes are on the object ball.

How to Aim

In the game of pocket billiards your "target," your point of aim, can be determined with mathematical accuracy for *every single shot*.

To determine your target do this: From the center of the pocket for which you are aiming, draw an imaginary line running back toward you dead through the "object ball." This is the ball you intend to pocket by hitting it with the cue ball (without also pocketing the cue ball, of course). Your target is located precisely where that line cuts through the object ball.

When you step up to the table to make your shot, first determine your target. Then strive to hit it. Sight down the intended path of the cue ball; your eyes stop at the object ball. Sight back and forth along that path until it becomes fixed in your mind.

At the moment they stroke, most players have their eyes fixed on the object ball. The great Willie Hoppe, however, used to look at the cue ball, last. Either way just be certain that your eyes remain fixed on one ball or the other until the follow-through of your stroke has been executed.

When you take aim and prepare to stroke, keep your head perfectly still. If you move it to the right or left, or up or down you are almost certain to miss your target.

One last bit of advice: concentrate. When you sight your target, it should demand your full attention.

I sight down the intended path of the cue ball.

*The arrows indicate the target, the point of aim,
for each of these side pocket shots.*

I sight down the intended path of the cue ball; at the moment of my stroke, my eyes are on the object ball.

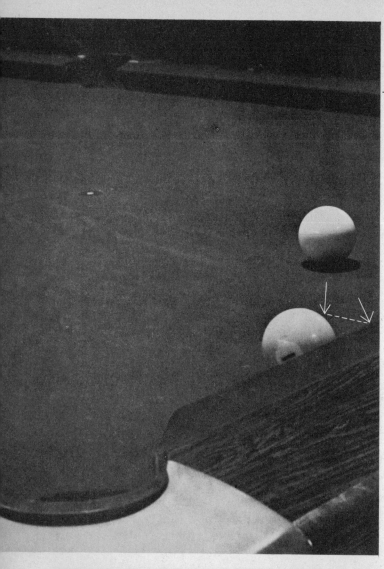

How to Aim
for Rail Shots

Rail shots—those where the object ball is touching ("frozen") to the rail—are an exception to the targeting rule. Here you must aim to strike the object ball and rail at the same time.

When you do this, the object ball will move along the rail, almost cling to it, in fact, until the ball drops into the pocket.

Sometimes imparting english toward the pocket side of the cue ball (in this instance, right english) is a good idea (see page 35). It helps assure the object ball will hug the rail.

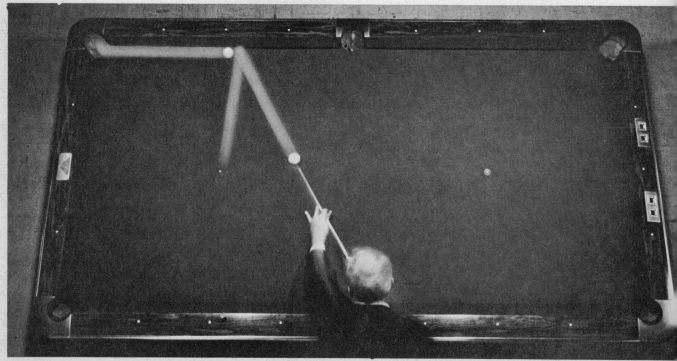

Rail combinations (when the object ball pockets another ball) are no problem. Just be sure the balls are frozen to the cushion. Then strike the object ball and the cushion simultaneously. Stroke the dead center of the cue ball.

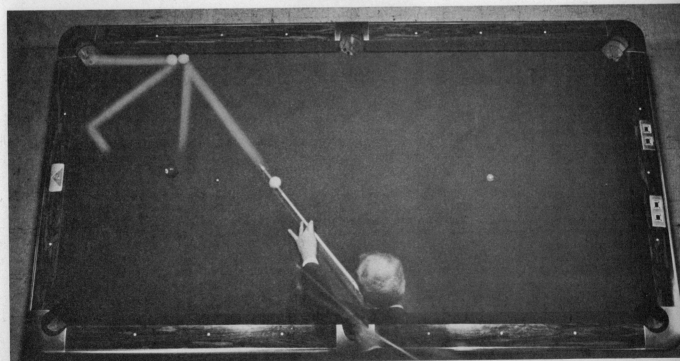

How to Use the Mechanical Bridge

Once in a while you will find the cue ball and the object ball are so far away from you that you will have to resort to the use of the mechanical bridge. (Sometimes this piece of equipment is called a "rake" and sometimes a "stick bridge.")

Place the mechanical bridge just as you would your hand bridge—six to eight inches from the cue ball. Keep the butt end of the bridge stick to your left and flat on the table. Hold it firm with your left hand.

Your head should position directly over your cue, just as in any conventional shot. Don't stab at the ball; stroke it smoothly.

When shooting over obstructing balls that are too far to reach without a mechanical bridge, turn the head of the bridge on its side to get the necessary elevation.

Rail Bridges

When the cue ball is frozen to the rail, I rest my fingers and the tip of my thumb on the rail; I guide the cue through the pocket formed by the thumb and forefinger.

When the cue ball is 2 to 3 inches off the rail, I move my hand forward and stroke the cue over my thumb and between the middle and index fingers.

When the cue ball's about six to eight inches off the rail, I use a bridge like the conventional one. However, I use the rail to support my wrist and the heel of my hand.

The Flat-Hand Bridge

At times when I am seeking to get a lot of speed, or follow, on the ball, I sometimes resort to a flat-hand bridge. With this, the fingers and thumb are flat on the table and can do nothing to impede the speed of the stroke.

The flat-hand bridge is sometimes useful when you have to lean out over the table to reach the cue ball. In cases like this the flat-hand bridge, is often the only way you can get really solid support for your cue.

When using the flat-hand bridge, the cue is stroked through the shallow pocket formed by the thumb and forefinger.

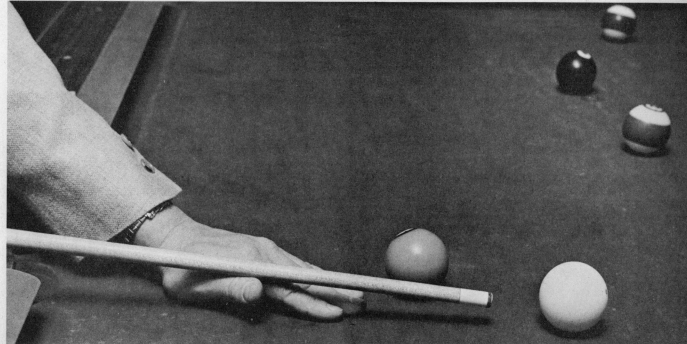

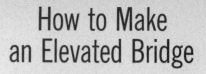

When forced to stroke over an obstructing ball or balls, I use an elevated bridge. To form one, I simply place my fist on the table, fifth finger down, about an inch or so in back of the obstructing ball. I cross my thumb over my forefinger and then stroke through the pocket they form.

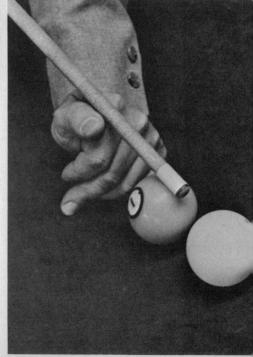

When you shoot over an obstructing ball, you have to strike downward to hit the cue ball solidly. You will have to change your stance as above, your weight principally on your left foot.

How to Shoot Left-Handed Shots

Newspaper stories have called me ambidextrous. I'm really not. I am a natural right-hander, but I have found an easy way to shoot left-handed, so easy it makes me look like a natural southpaw.

I simply form my right hand into a fist and place it flat on the table. Then I make an opening between the thumb and forefinger, and I stroke the cue through that opening. To me, this is a perfectly natural way to execute shots that call for a left-handed style. Try it.

HOW TO CONTROL THE CUE BALL

One aspect of pocket billiards play usually separates the pro from the amateur. The professional always knows where the cue ball is going; the amateur knows some of the time but not all of the time.

What action the cue ball will take is based on a number of factors. First of all, it depends on the speed and force of your stroke. It also depends on exactly *where* on the ball the tip of the cue strikes it.

It can strike the cue ball high or low, to the left or to the right, or you can make the tip strike dead center. Each of these hits gives a different type of "english."

"English" the dictionary defines as "the spinning motion of the ball." This spinning motion has a profound influence over the path that the cue ball will take on its way to the object ball. It also influences the path the object ball will take after it is struck by the cue ball. Learning how to employ english is your first step in learning how to control the cue ball.

The Centerball Stroke

Approximately 40 to 50 per cent of the shots you'll be faced with in the average game of pocket billiards demand no more than a simple centerball stroke. This is just what its name implies, a stroke that hits the cue ball dead center.

After the ball is struck, the cue follows through for three or four inches along the line of the stroke. Never overlook this final part of the stroke.

The centerball stroke also serves as a stop-ball stroke: Strike firmly, snap your follow-through, and the cue ball will stop in its tracks after it hits the object ball.

Another characteristic of centerball stroking is well worth noting. As you step up the speed of the cue ball you *decrease the angle* the object ball will take after it strikes the cushion. As the cue ball's speed is slowed, *this angle increases.*

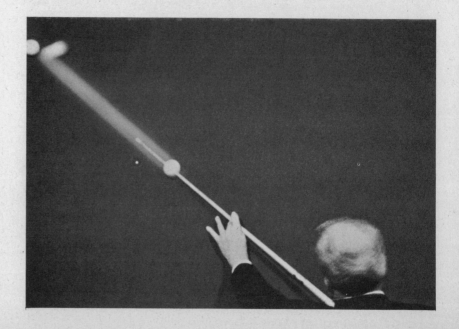

*Facing page: This centerball stroke is also serving as a stop-ball stroke.
Note how the cue ball has stopped, rolling only slightly to its right
after hitting the object ball. This picture shows perfect aim for a centerball stroke.*

TARGET
AREA

How to Apply Draw

The draw shot imparts *reverse english* to the cue ball. It makes it roll back toward you after it strikes the object ball.

To make it draw, strike the cue ball below center. The lower you go, the more draw you will get—simply raise or lower your finger bridge.

Cue tip will strike the lower half of the cue ball in this draw shot.
Facing page: a typical draw shot. It's important to keep the cue parallel to the table.
If you lower the cue tip by raising the butt end of the stick you won't get
as much draw as you will if you keep the stick parallel to the table, or as nearly parallel as you can.

TARGET
AREA

How to Apply Follow

"Follow" is the term applied to the method of stroking that forces the cue ball to move in the same direction as the object ball after the object ball has been struck.

Follow english is accomplished by simply striking the cue ball above center. The higher you hit the ball, the greater the follow.

A smooth follow-through is extremely important in achieving the proper follow stroke.

I often employ the flat-hand bridge when using follow. With it, I can follow through with the greatest ease and I can keep the cue almost perfectly level throughout the stroke.

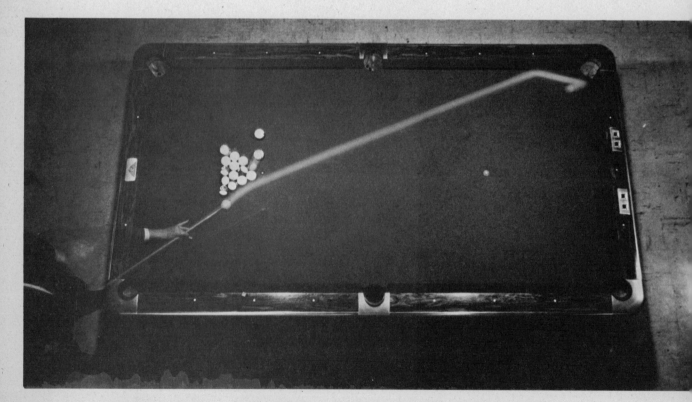

The path of the cue ball in a follow shot demonstrating a safety—a defensive maneuver which tries to leave the opponent without a reasonable shot.
Facing page: in a follow shot the cue tip strikes the upper half of the cue ball.

English to the Right or Left

As we have seen, english is applied to make the cue ball draw or follow. *Right english*—the cue tip striking the cue ball to *right* of its center—makes the ball go to the right. *Left english*—the cue tip striking the cue ball to *left* of its center—makes it go to the left.

English has other effects on the cue ball. It will add speed to a ball after it hits a cushion; it will also increase the angle the ball takes after hitting a cushion.

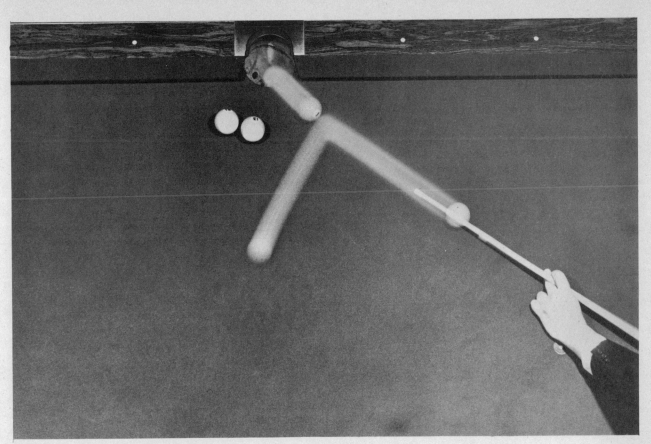

Using left draw english, I make the cue ball arc to the left.

A demonstration of english to the right

Cue ball "stops" after striking and holing object ball,
and gains position for corner pocket shot.

HOW TO PLAY FOR POSITION

Billiards is a game of thinking ahead. You must not only play to make the shot at hand, you must play the next shot too. By this I mean you must be able to control the cue ball to such a degree that you can bring it into a pre-planned place on the table following your stroke.

Such thinking ahead is "playing position."

Don't underestimate the importance of position play. In stressing its extreme value to beginners, I tell them that if they miss their position, they are only too likely to miss their upcoming shot. It's as important to get good position for the next shot as it is to hole the ball you're striving for.

Using Stop for Position

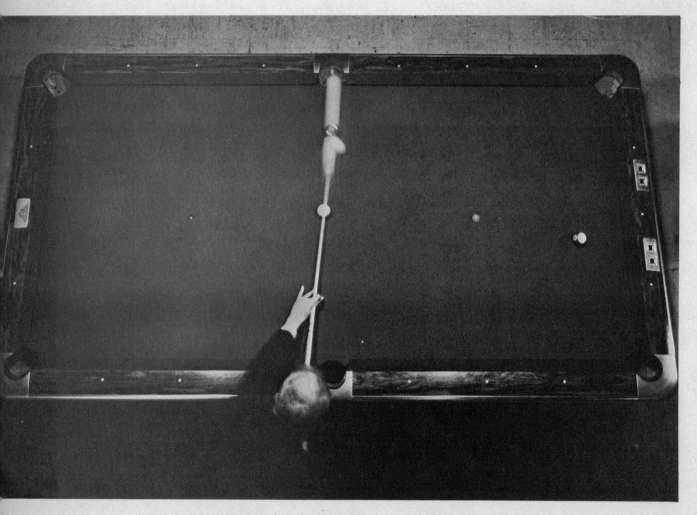

*Cue ball "stops" after striking and holing object ball,
and gains position for corner pocket shot.*

Using Follow for Position

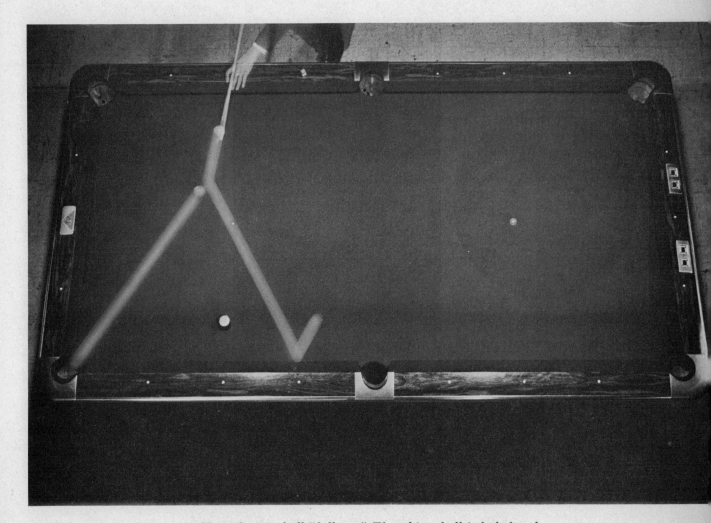

Here the cue ball "follows." The object ball is holed and perfect position is gained for the upcoming shot.

Using Draw for Position

The cue ball is stroked with draw, or reverse english.
The object ball is banked into the near side pocket;
the cue ball gains perfect position for the upcoming corner pocket shot.

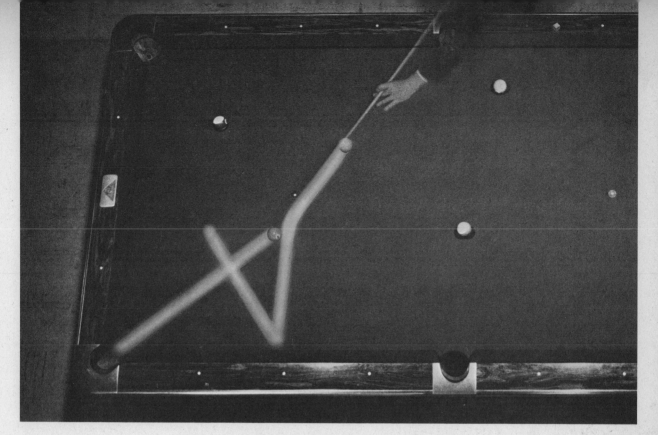

Using Right Follow for Position

Right-hand follow serves to increase the cue ball's rebound angle so that it gains position for corner pocket shot. Note how continuous-sequence camera indicates precisely where I struck the cue ball by indicating how the cue might have pierced the ball.

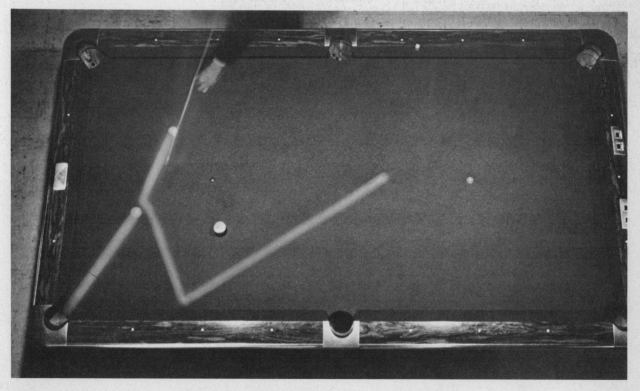

Using Left Follow for Position

Here left-hand follow is used to increase the cue ball's rebound angle.

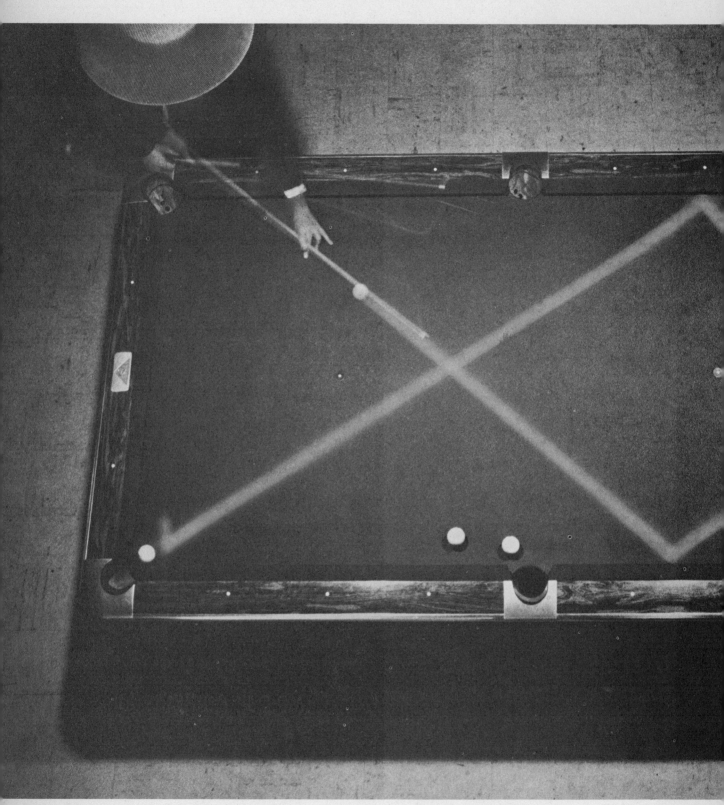

Not for beginners: a difficult three-cushion carom shot

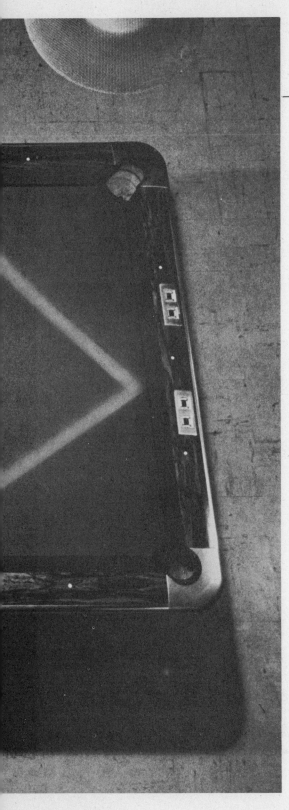

ADVANCED SHOOTING

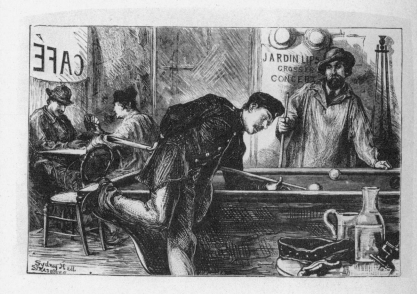

Bank Shot from a Side Rail

In attempting a bank shot, you aim so that the object ball will strike a target on the cushion opposite the pocket for which it is intended. Bank shots are difficult. You seldom see them attempted even in championship play.

In determining your target you have to "bisect the angle." Here's what that means. In the situation shown in this picture the object ball is on an imaginary line extending between the diamond on the rail just to the left of the side pocket and the diamond opposite it across the table. Now draw an imaginary line from the object ball to the diamond in the foreground and another imaginary line from the object ball to the side pocket in the foreground. When stroking you try to bisect (cut in two) the angle formed by these two lines.

On bank shots like this, stroke the ball with medium speed; use no english. In other words, strive to keep the object ball's rebound angle a normal one.

Bank Shot from an End Rail

Banking a ball from one of the end rails into a corner pocket is even more difficult to do. Because of the greater distance the object ball has to travel, there is much more margin for error.

Again, as in the bank shot from the side rail, you determine the path your ball must travel by "bisecting the angle."

In the picture on this page the object ball went into the pocket out of sight on my left, while the cue ball, as you can see, was given just enough draw to place it smack in front of the corner pocket in the foreground.

Frozen Combinations

This combination is "frozen," the object balls touching one another.

On setups of this type, once you determine the second object ball (the one nearest the pocket) is on a direct path to the pocket, the rest is simple. Just stroke the cue ball so it hits in the center of the first object ball. Use a centerball stroke.

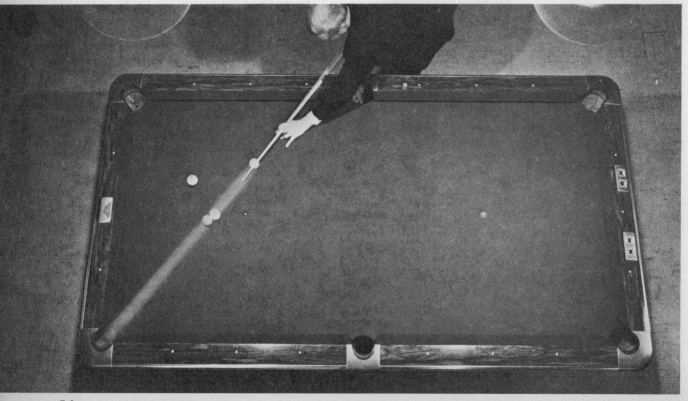

Two-Ball Combinations

Combination shots like this take some planning.

Here is how this shot was made. First, I determined a point of aim on the 5 ball. Next, I determined a point of aim on the 1 ball that would bring it into contact with the 5 ball target.

In stroking the cue ball, I used a medium centerball stroke.

Multiple Combinations

For multiple ball combinations you determine a point of aim for each ball. Begin with the ball nearest to the pocket and work your way back toward the cue ball.

Link the targets with a very cautious stroke. The slightest degree of error means you will miss the shot.

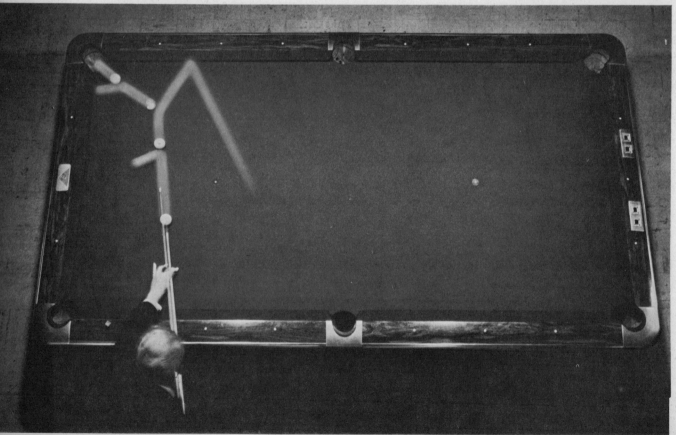

The Kiss Shot

Only with experience will you come to recognize prospective kiss shots in which the called ball caroms off an object ball into the pocket.

You tell when a kiss shot is "on" if you can extend a line drawn between the two balls to the middle of the pocket. Then you can be sure the shot can be made.

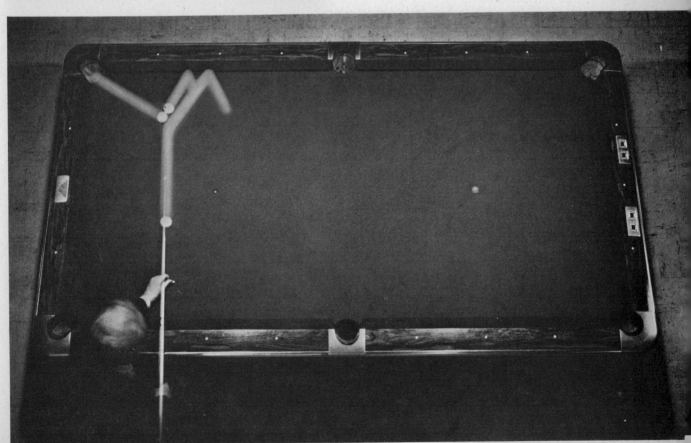

The opening break shot in a game of 14.1 Continuous billiards.

A GAME OF BILLIARDS

"Fourteen-one Continuous" is the classic game of pocket billiards. Throughout the years it is the style of play that has been used in championship competition. It pits one player directly against the other, calling upon each contestant to use every facet of his ability. For player and spectator it is pocket billiards at its exciting best.

In 14.1 Continuous, a player receives one point for each ball "called" and pocketed. In championship play, the first player to score 150 points wins the game.

Play is conducted in innings. One inning is a playing turn by each of the two players. A player continues with his turn or inning until he fouls or misses a shot.

During his inning, each player attempts to pocket all the balls on the table but one. If he accomplishes this, the 14 that have been pocketed are racked again and the ball that remains on the table becomes the "break ball." Play continues. (It is from this aspect of the game the name "14.1" is derived. The "14" refers to the 14 balls that are racked, the "1" refers to the break ball.)

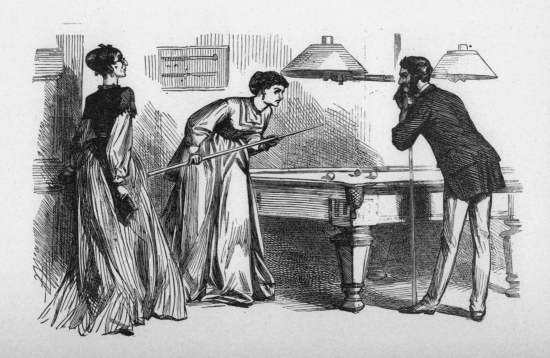

The Opening Break

On the break in a game of 14.1 Continuous, you have two choices. You can call a ball and pocket it, or play it safe by driving two object balls to the cushions. Invariably players elect to play it safe (see glossary in back of book).

On the opening break when you send two balls to the cushions, you try to leave your opponent no choice but to play it safe also—and thereby regain the play yourself.

Here is how it's done. With a slight right english, you aim to stroke the cue ball into the ball at the right corner of the triangular-racked setup. You aim to hit this ball very "thin" (barely nicking it).

This sends the ball on the right corner to the rear cushion, the ball on the left corner to the side cushion.

The cue ball rebounds to a frozen or near-frozen position against the head rail, or to a frozen position between the sides of the left-hand corner pocket at the head of the table. Either way your opponent has no choice but to play a safety.

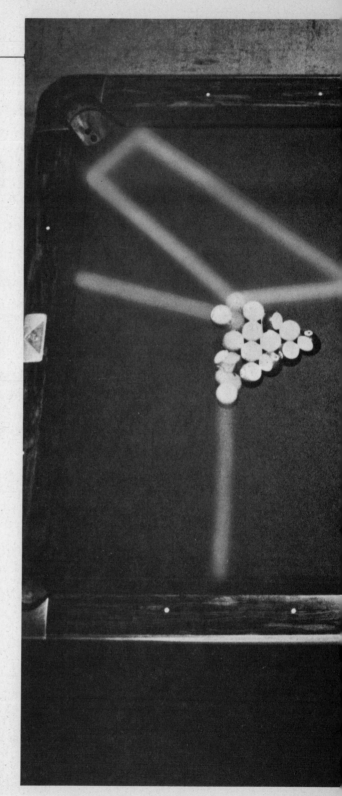

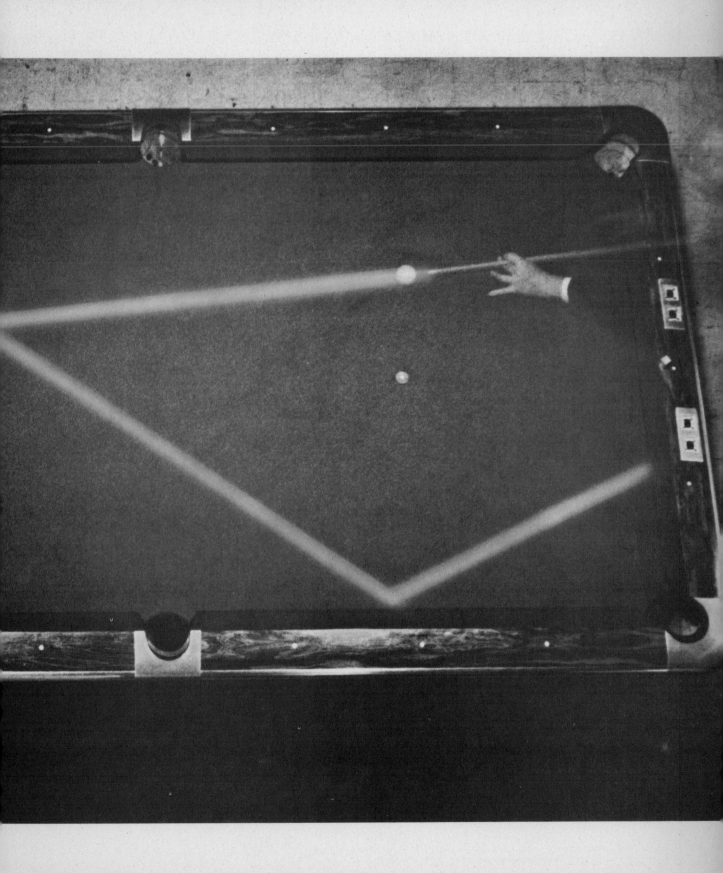

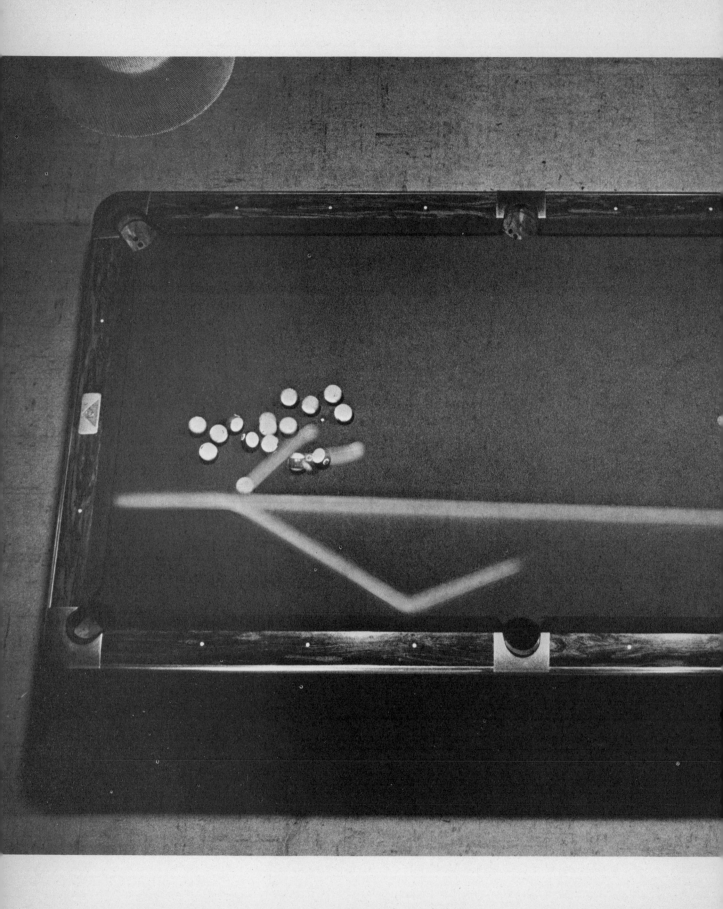

A Safety Situation

If your opponent has the opening shot, he may leave you with no alternative but to play a return safety off the clustered balls. (The requirements of safety play demand that you either send an object ball to a cushion or cause the cue ball to contact a cushion after hitting an object ball.)

Most players play the return safety as shown here. The cue ball strikes the side rail, then the foot rail and then glances gently off the clustered balls so as not to dislodge any of them from the pack. Then the cue ball returns to a position close by the foot rail. The opposition is left without a reasonable shot.

The return safety after your opponent's opening shot can be played in the manner shown here. The cue ball caroms and hits into the rack driving two balls to the rail (as specified by the rules), but buries itself among the clustered balls leaving the opposing player without a reasonable shot.

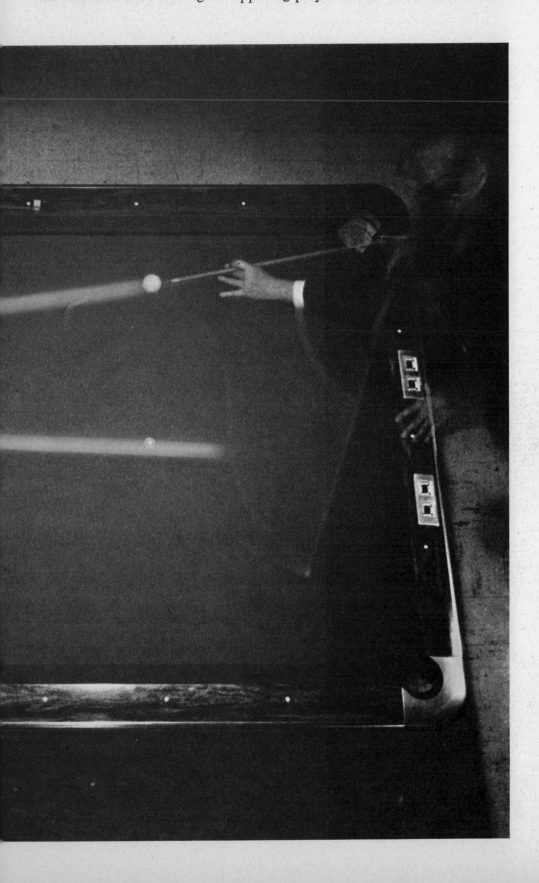

Break Situation 1

This is the classic break shot. The object ball is easily holed in the corner pocket; the cue ball caroms off the break ball to knife into the cluster and spread the balls about the table.

Stroke the cue ball with follow to get optimum results.

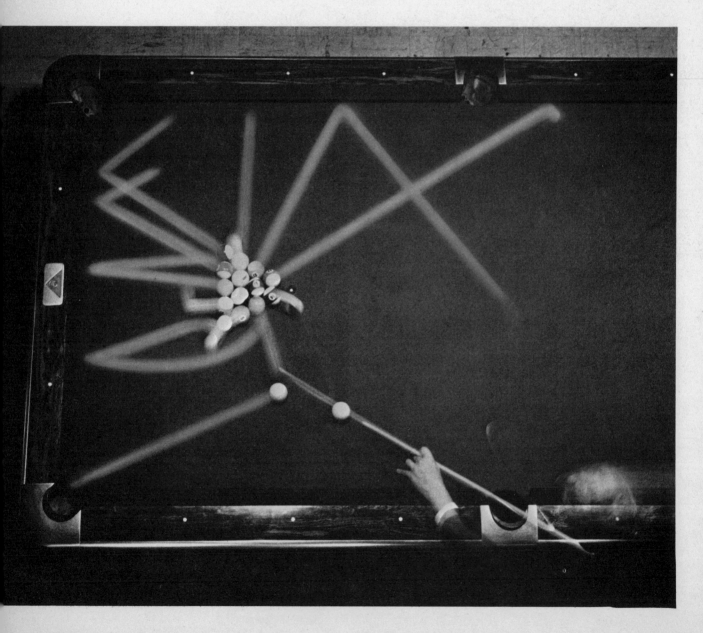

Break Situation 2

When the break ball is positioned behind the racked balls the object ball is holed in the corner pocket. Then the cue ball strikes the bottom of the cluster and caroms to the side rail.

Again, follow is recommended.

Break Situation 3

Here is a side pocket break. The object ball offers no problem; the trick is to get the proper cushion carom. Left english on the cue ball helps.

Break Situation 4

This one isn't for beginners. The cue ball is struck with left english and a smart follow stroke. When the shot is executed properly, the cue ball will loop off the rail into the rack with almost amazing speed.

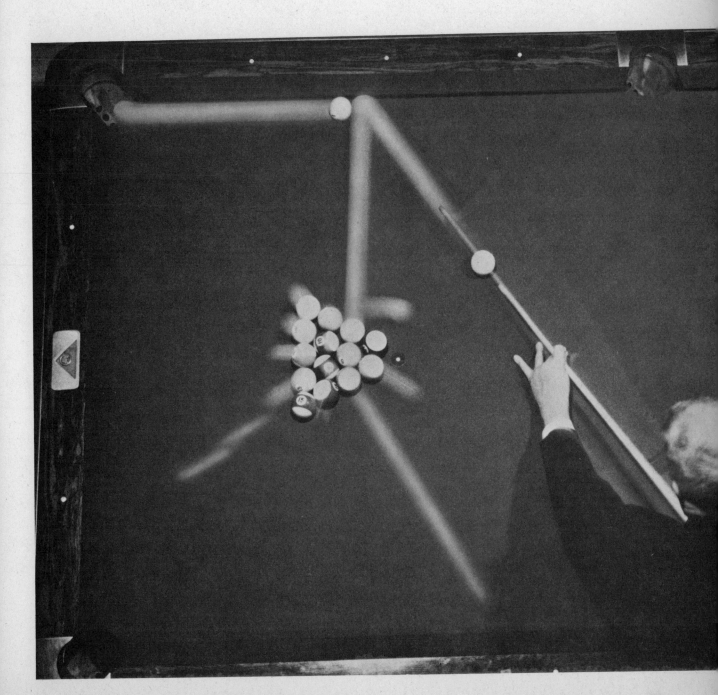

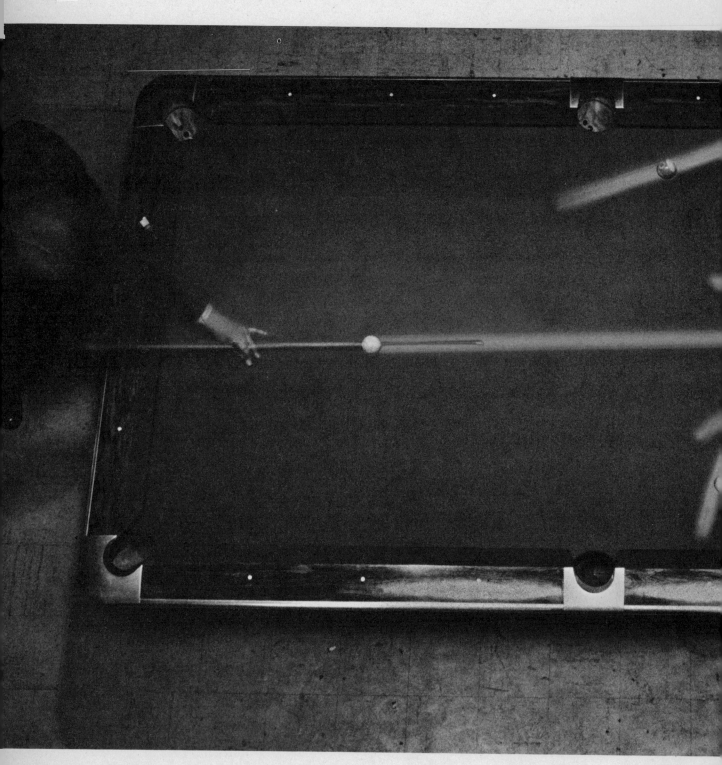

An overhead view of a break shot that would be appropriate for a game of Rotation or a game of Eight-Ball in which the player gets credit for any balls pocketed on the break. Note carefully where I position the cue ball to get optimum power. I strike the cue ball with high follow for a shot like this.

Rotation and Eight-Ball

Youngsters and beginning billiards players of all ages enjoy Rotation. It doesn't require as much skill or experience as 14.1 Continuous, and it can be played by two, three or four people at a time.

The balls are racked in a triangle, the 1 ball at the apex, the 2 and 3 balls in the corners.

Beginning with the 1 ball, the players must pocket balls in numerical order. They receive a point for each shot equal to the numerical designation of the pocketed ball (the 1 ball is worth one point; the 6 ball, six points, etc.). The first player or team to score 61 points wins the game.

The first shooter aims for the 1 ball in his attempt to spread the rack. He is credited with any balls that are pocketed on the break, so he tries to make the shot as powerful as he can.

Eight-ball is another popular pocket billiards game, especially among the young.

The balls are racked in a triangle, and the eight ball is placed in the center of the triangle.

One player or team is designated to pocket balls numbered 1 through 7; the other player or team must pocket balls 9 through 15.

After a player pockets all the balls in his grouping, he is allowed to shoot the 8 ball. If he calls the 8 and pockets it, he wins.

As in Rotation, the first shooter is credited with any balls pocketed on the break.

The Opening Break in Nine-Ball

Nine-Ball is another exciting game. It is played with balls numbered 1 through 9 racked in a diamond shape for the opening break.

The object of the game is to call and pocket the balls in sequence. The player that calls and pockets the 9 ball wins.

Placement of the cue ball on the Nine-Ball break shot is similar to that for the Eight-Ball or Rotation break shots. The continuous-sequence photograph shows the balls both as they lay racked and as they scattered when the cue ball hit into them.

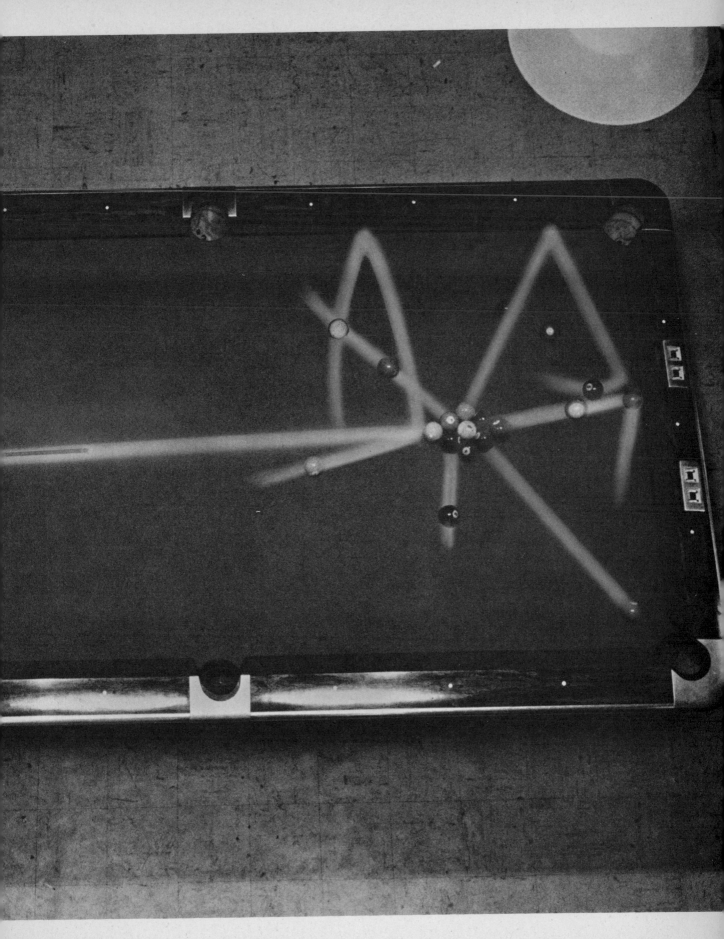

I devote some part of each day to practice drills like this one.

HOW TO PRACTICE

If you want to become skilled at pocket billiards you must practice. There is no substitute for it.

Even the best professional players practice. Before a tournament they will schedule long hours of practice drills every day for a week or more. And if you have ever seen a championship tournament you know that a special practice table is set up for the players close by the tournament site. What's more, it's used!

Your own practice should be something more than the experience you get in competitive billiard play. You should schedule special practice sessions where you drill yourself on the weaker points in your game.

These drills need not be long ones, but if you want them to have value for you schedule them regularly. Practicing on a schedule of even twice a week can be very helpful.

This section presents some practice drills that may be useful to you. Study them—try them!

Draw Practice

This drill is an excellent one for practicing position play by using draw english.

Arrange a series of balls in a semicircle about a side pocket. Then pocket each ball, moving from right to left. The trick is to use draw to gain position each time for the next shot.

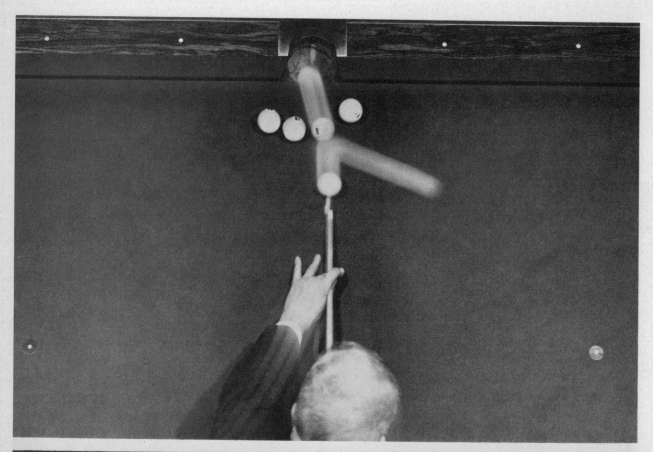

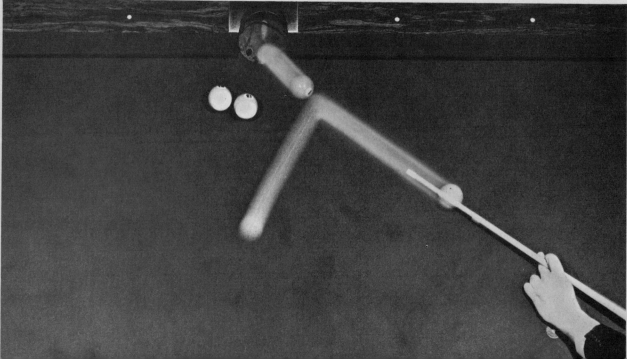

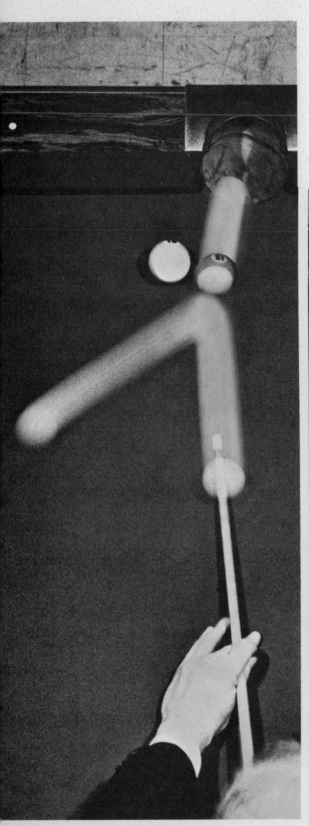

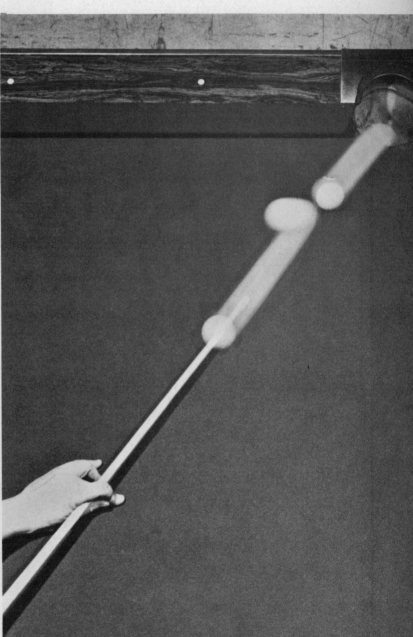

Speed Drill

In pocket billiards, the speed of the cue ball and object ball is often just as important to the shot as ball direction. This drill is designed to help you become an astute judge of ball speed.

Lay a sheet of paper at one end of the table. Place an object ball at the same end of the table. Try to rebound it from the rail opposite on to the square of paper. Practice the same drill across side rails.

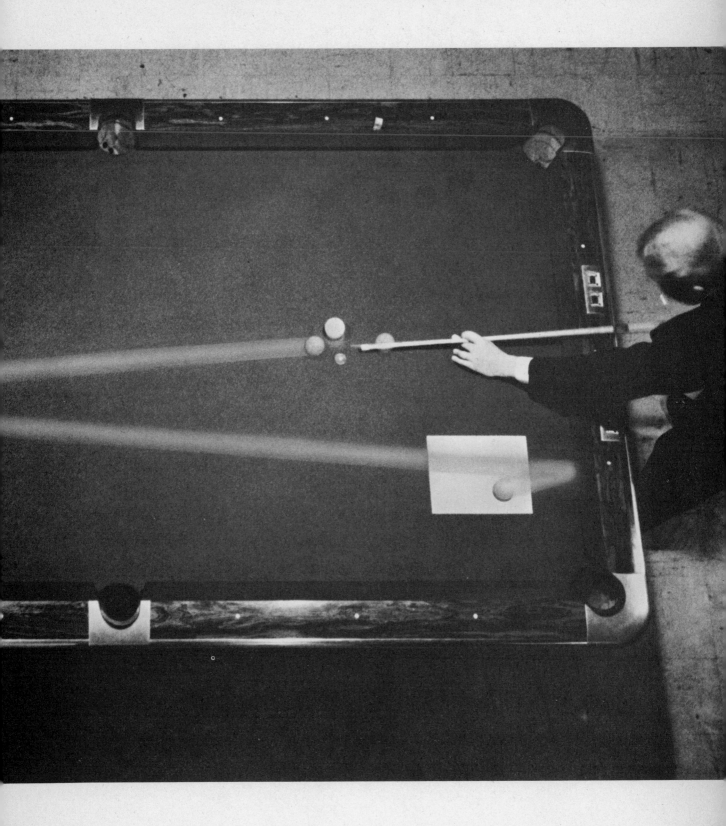

Point-of-Aim Drill

To become expert in quickly and accurately determining your target on the object ball, this practice drill will help you.

Line up a series of balls at one end of the table. Stroke each into a corner pocket near the side opposite.

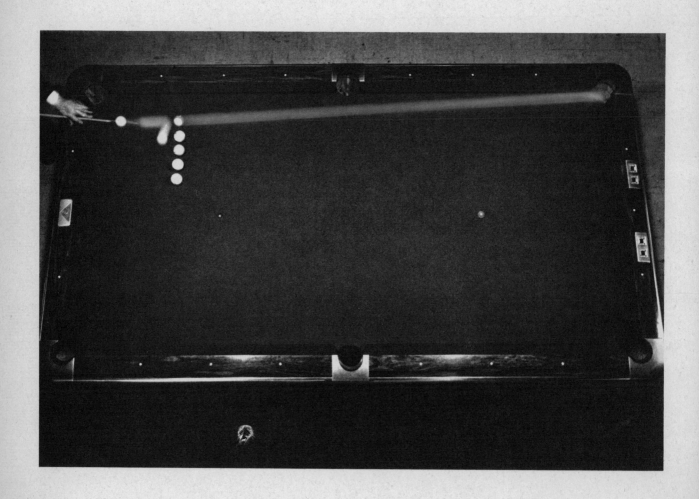

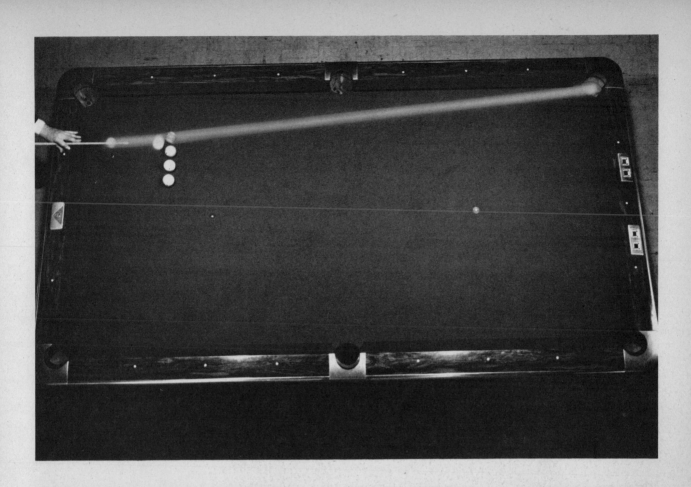

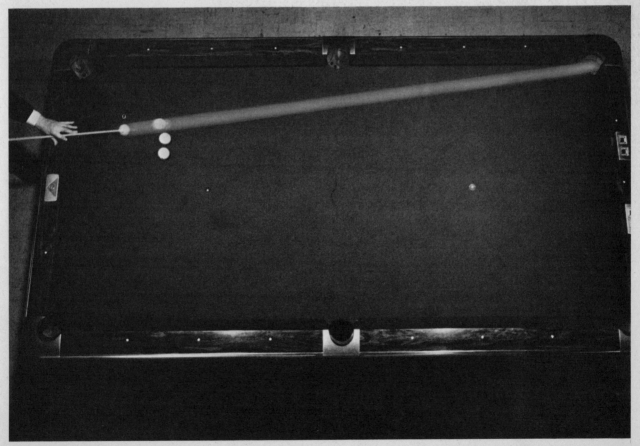

Trick Shots

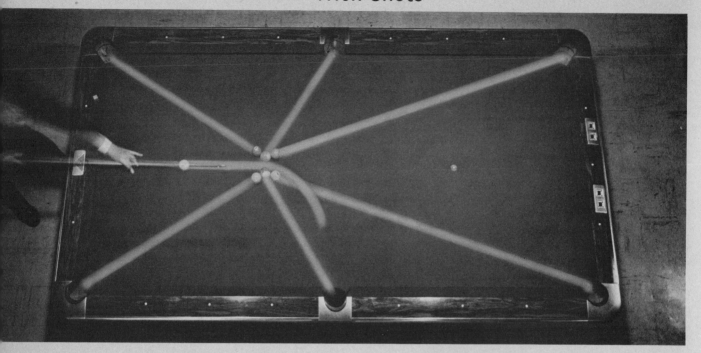

Holing six balls with one shot (above) is easy—if you know how. Notice how the center balls of the spread are positioned on a line with the diamonds closest to the side pockets. I use high follow english. Trick shot below is called the Football Shot. Eleven balls are arranged as shown. Using high follow, aim the cue ball between the first two balls of the setup. Down the line, the balls will ricochet into one another. The last ball of the setup will be pocketed.

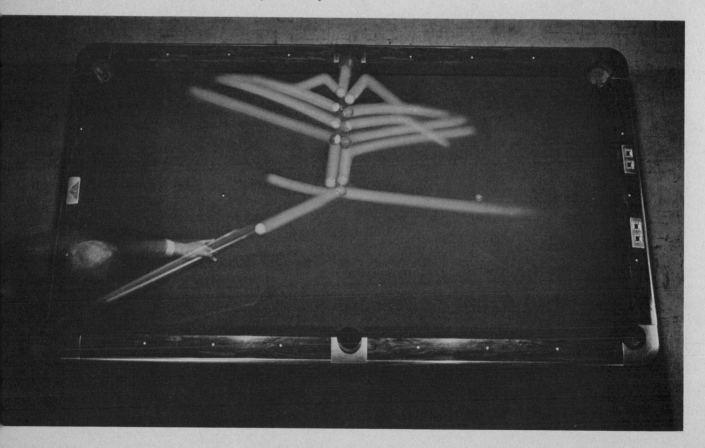

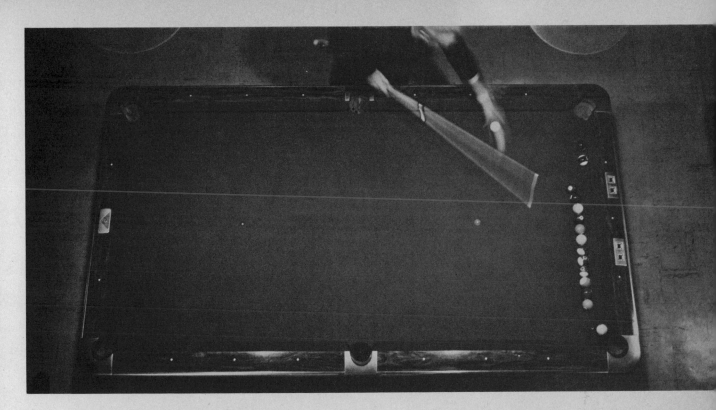

This is exciting to watch. It's called the Machine Gun Shot. Arrange a setup of balls as shown above. I aim the cue ball between the first two balls of the setup (those frozen to the rail). I use hard right english. The second object ball (the second one from the upper-right pocket) ricochets down the channel formed by the line of balls and into the corner pocket knocking out of the way every single ball in the line.

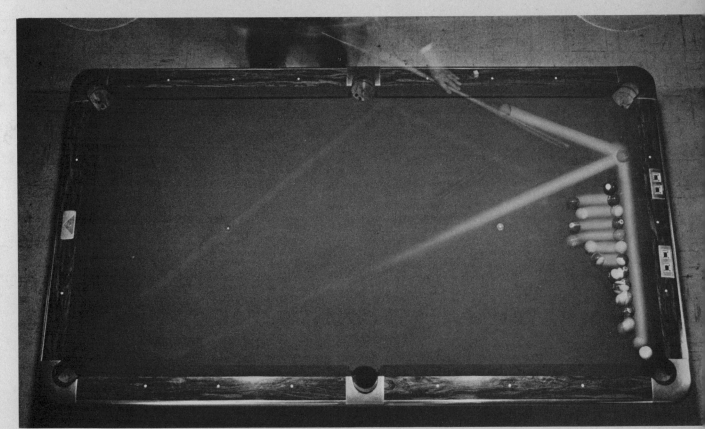

Ivory balls were in general use for centuries, and cost many a poor elephant his tusks. Balls molded of man-made materials began to appear in the 1880's. Today a good set of pocket billiard balls of the correct tournament weight costs $30.

EQUIPMENT
The Table

One indication of the growing popularity of pocket billiards is the wide variety of tables you see displayed at stores for purchase for home use. These range widely in size and in price.

You can buy a table as small as 20″ x 40″. Of course, the standard or championship table is a great deal larger than that—it measures 4½ x 9 feet. That's the size table you use at billiard centers. If you have the budget and if you have the room, buy this size; it's the one from which you'll get the most enjoyment.

On a standard size table, the playing surface should be 30 or 31 inches from the floor. The corner pockets should have openings of from 4⅞″ to 5⅛″; the side pockets should have openings of from 5⅜″ to 5⅝″.

If you are planning on buying a table for your home, be mindful that you need a good deal of clearance on each side of the table so players can properly position themselves for shots. In fact, if the standard 57″ cue is used, a five-foot clearance is necessary on all sides.

How much do tables cost? Prices begin at $100 and range to ten times that amount depending upon size, quality and accessories. And if you want a table just like the one at your local billiard center, prepare to pay about $1,500 for it. Today's billiard tables have lost the elephantine quality they had a few decades ago. They are framed in bright plastic hues and can be ordered with felt in decorator colors. Some models for home use feature board covers that convert them to dining or utility tables.

In striking contrast to the Victorian billiard table at left, today's sleek modern ones sport such features as built-in storage shelves for balls and built-in markers for keeping score. The fabric covering the slate playing surface, traditionally dark green, is now available in blue, gold or tangerine — to the horror of old-time pool players, perhaps, but the delight of the many women who have taken up the game in recent years.

The Cue

Whether you are purchasing a cue for home use, or merely choosing one for an evening's use from the rack at your billiard center, it is important to select a stick that suits you in both weight and length.

Don't choose a cue that is too light. Rather, try to have a little heft to your cue so that when you stroke the ball the stick will do some work for you. If you are of average height and build, a 19-ounce stick should be about right. For youngsters, a stick of 14 to 15 ounces suits.

Length is less of a consideration because most sticks available to you will be 57 inches long. For junior players there are cues of 4 feet and even 3 feet lengths that can be purchased.

Before you begin your game, roll the cue on a table or a countertop. If the stick rolls easily, you know it's a straight one. If the cue arches up as you roll it, you can be sure it's bowed; you won't be able to hit accurately with it. Select another.

Also, before you begin, stroke the cue through your finger bridge. Be certain that you can stroke it smoothly, that it doesn't stick.

Examine the cue stick's leather tip. It should be no smaller or larger than the flat tip end of the stick. The edges of the leather tip should be rounded.

When storing your cue, keep it in a cool dry place. Dampness can cause a wooden cue to warp. Also, store the stick perfectly upright. Stand it flush to a wall; don't let it lean.

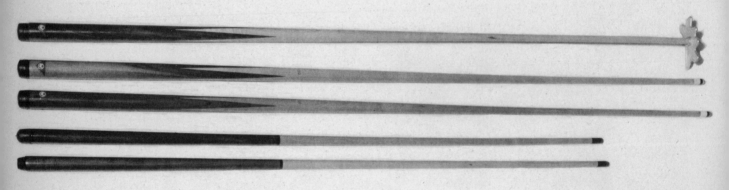

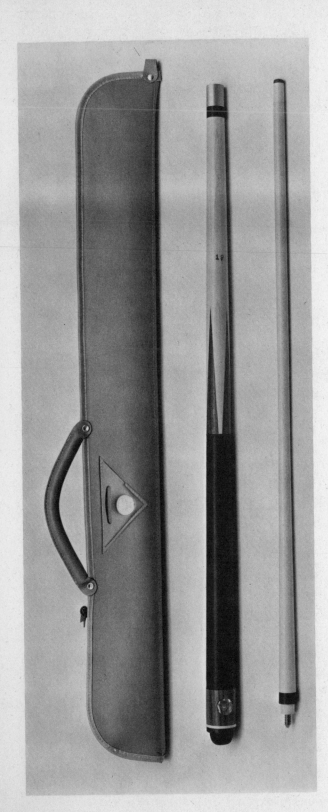

The Custom Cue

A pocket billiard professional and anyone at all, in fact, who becomes really serious about the sport, purchases a custom cue, one that in weight, length and taper feels perfectly suited to him.

Most of these custom cues are "jointed." They break down into two sections for easy carrying and easy storage.

A good quality jointed cue costs about $25, although professionals pay up to $100 and sometimes more for theirs. Billiard supply stores also sell carrying cases for your cue stick. These cost about five dollars.

Toward the turn of the century championship matches drew great crowds.

glossary

Angle—The relationship of the cue ball to the cushion.

Ball On—A ball is said to be "on the pocket" if it can be driven into a called pocket on a combination shot.

Bank—A rebound from a cushion.

Bank Shot—One wherein the object ball is rebounded from one or more cushions before pocketing.

Break—In all billiard games, the opening shot.

Bridge—The placement of the left hand (for right-handed players) on the table for the purpose of guiding the cue.

Bridge, Mechanical—The cue-like device with a notched plate at the tip end; used as a "bridge" in executing those shots where the conventional hand bridge will not serve.

Called Ball—The ball a player announces he intends to pocket.

Called Pocket—The pocket into which the player announces he intends to drop a called ball.

Carom—The action of deflecting one ball from another or from a ball to a cushion or cushions.

Center Spot—A spot in the precise center of the table on which the cue ball or an object ball may be spotted.

Cue Ball In Hand—Said of a player who puts the cue ball in play at a point of his choice within the head string, usually as a result of a foul or an error on the part of his opponent.

Cuing—Striking the cue ball with the cue.

Cushion—The cloth-covered, resilient rail that borders the pocket billiards table.

Dead Ball—One that stops dead upon contact with another ball.

Diamond—One of the 18 small white plastic inlays inserted in the flat wooden rails of the billiard table that aid as targets in shot making.

Draw—A stroking technique in which the cue ball, stroked below center, reverses its path after striking the object ball.

English—Spin imparted to the cue ball by striking it to the left or right of center; or above or below center.

Follow—A stroking technique in which the cue ball is struck above center; makes the cue ball "follow" the same general direction as the object ball.

Foot Rail—The short rail of a table which does not bear the manufacturer's name plate.

Foot Spot—A spot at the foot end of the table; lies equidistant between the table's center spot and the center diamond on the foot rail.

Foot String—Line drawn through the foot spot and the center diamonds of the side rails (toward the foot of the table.)

Foul—Any infraction of the rules.

Frozen—Term used to describe balls that are touching one another on the table.

Head Rail—The short rail of the table which bears the manufacturer's name plate.

Head Spot—A spot at the head end of the table; lies equidistant between the table's center spot and the center diamond on the head rail.

Head String—Line drawn through the head spot and the center diamonds of the side rails (toward the head of the table).

High Run—The highest consecutive series of points or scores in one inning of a game.

Inning—A player's turn at the table.

Kiss Shot—A type of carom shot (see page 57).

Lagging—The practice of banking the balls over the full length of the table (from head rail to foot rail); used to determine rotation of play.

Massé—Application of extreme english on the cue ball; used to drive the cue ball around an object ball.

Miscue—A stroke in which the cue tip slips from the cue ball; any faulty stroke.

Nominated Ball—A called ball.

Rack—The wooden or plastic triangular-shaped frame into which the balls are placed; also refers to the grouped balls themselves (without the rack).

Rail—The flat surfaces of the table above the table bed from which the cushions slope.

Run—A series of consecutive scores or points in one inning.

Safety—A defensive effort, one in which a player sacrifices an opportunity to score in an attempt to leave his opponent without a reasonable shot.

Scratch—An unanticipated development which incurs a penalty such as loss of turn. Most often it occurs when the cue ball is unintentionally "scratched" into a pocket.

Setup—An easy shot.

Spot—See head, foot, center spots.

Spot Shot—A stroke in which the player shoots at a ball that has been placed on a spot.

Spotting—The placement or replacement of balls on the table as required by the rules of the game.

PLAYING RULES
AND
REGULATIONS

Introduction

Rotation, Eight-Ball, and 14.1 Continuous Billiards rank today as the most popular of the many types of pocket billiard games played throughout the country. The rules and regulations that govern the play of these games are given here. They were developed in co-operation with the Billiard Room Proprietors Association of America.

In many cases, the rules and regulations that govern pocket billiard play are modified by local or house rules. Be aware of these rule modifications before you compete in any type of match or tournament play.

14.1 CONTINUOUS BILLIARDS

The game of 14.1 Continuous Billiards is the sport's classic game. It is the style of play used in competition in all pocket billiard championship contests. It is the ideal game for head-to-head billiards competition, for it calls upon each individual player to use every facet of his ability.

Section 1, Equipment

The game is played with a cue ball and fifteen object balls.

The balls are racked in a triangle at the foot of the table, with the 15 ball placed at the top of the triangle (facing the starting player) on the foot spot. The 1 ball is placed at the left-hand corner of the triangle; the 5 ball is placed at the right-hand corner of the triangle. The higher numbered balls are placed toward the top of the triangle, and the lower numbered balls are arranged toward the base or lower part of the triangle.

Section 2, Object of the Game

A player receives one point for each ball "called" and pocketed. (The player must designate each ball he intends to pocket and call the pocket in which he intends to hole the ball.) Also, the player receives one point for every ball pocketed in addition to the designated ball. In championship play, the first player to score 150 points wins the game.

Play is conducted in innings. An inning is made up of the playing turns of opposing players. A player continues with his turn or inning until he fouls or until he misses a shot.

Section 3, Opening (or Break) Shot

Contestants lag to determine honors for break. Each, in turn, strokes the cue ball from any location within the head string, to the foot cushion and return. The player whose stroke stops the cue ball nearest to the head rail wins the lag. Then he may break the rack of balls, or assign the break to his opponent.

The starting player, on his opening stroke, may position the cue ball anywhere within the head string. On the opening shot, he must send two or more object balls to the cushion, or else he must complete a called shot.

If the starting player fails to drive two balls to the cushion or pocket a called ball, his stroke is foul, and he is penalized two points. His opponent then has the choice of shooting, or he may, instead, compel the starting player to shoot again. (In this case the balls are re-racked.)

If the starting player fulfills the requirement of sending two object balls to the cushion, or if he pockets a called ball, but "scratches" the cue ball into a pocket, he loses his inning and is penalized one point. His opponent may then place the cue ball at any location within the head string in taking his shot.

Section 4, Play of the Game

On each shot or stroke, the player must complete one of three alternative actions. He must:

a. pocket the designated object ball.

b. make the cue ball strike the designated object ball and one other object ball, sending the second ball into a cushion or a pocket.

c. make the cue ball strike the designated object ball and then strike a cushion.

If a player fails to successfully complete his shot (a , above), he has made an error and his inning is completed. If he fails to complete the alternative cue ball caroms (b and c, above), he fouls. When a foul is levied, the player loses one turn and a one point penalty is assessed against him.

Section 5, Continuous Play

A player may pocket up to fourteen balls in succession, leaving a single object ball (plus the cue ball) on the table. The fourteen pocketed balls are then racked (a second cue ball is used in place of the fifteenth ball for the purpose of racking, and then removed once the triangular rack is removed).

After the fourteen balls are racked, play continues. The shooting player may aim at the newly racked balls or at the one remaining ball outside the rack, but he must shoot in accordance with the rules set down in Section 4.

In the case of a scratch, the player loses his inning and also loses one point. Should a player scratch on three succeeding innings, he is to be penalized an additional 15 points—totaling 18 points.

Section 6, Fouls

Failure to comply with the below listed rules constitutes a foul. A one-point penalty is to be levied against the offending player in each case.

a. When shooting, a player must have one foot touching the floor.

b. A player, or any part of the player's person or clothing must not interfere with the cue ball or any of the object balls in any way.

c. The cue ball must not be hit with such force that it is driven from the table. (If the designated object ball is driven from the table, no foul is committed. The player simply loses his inning. The errant ball is to be placed on the foot spot.)

d. A player must not stroke the cue ball while the cue ball, or any of the object balls, are spinning or in motion.

EIGHT-BALL

Section 1, Equipment

The game is played with a cue ball and 15 object balls, numbered from 1 through 15.

The balls are racked in a triangle at the foot spot, with the 8 ball racked in the center of the triangle.

Section 2, Object of the Game

The balls are divided between opposing players or teams. One player or team is designated to pocket balls numbered 1 through 7; the other player or team must pocket balls numbered 9 through 15. The player or team pocketing its designated numerical grouping of balls, and then legally pocketing the 8 ball, wins the game.

Section 3, Play of the Game

Contestants lag or draw lots to determine order of play.

The starting player may locate the cue ball anywhere within the head string.

If the starting player pockets one or more balls on the opening shot, he is given his choice of the high or low numerical grouping of balls. If the starting player fails to pocket a ball on his opening shot, his opponent accepts the balls as they are positioned and is given his choice of the high or low numerical grouping. Players are not assigned their respective groupings until a ball is pocketed.

Players are allowed to play combination shots off balls in opponent's numerical grouping, except in case of the 8 ball being the object ball.

If a player pockets an opponent's ball, the opponent is credited with the ball. If a player pockets only an opponent's ball and no balls of his own numerical grouping, it is a miss and the player loses his inning.

Section 4, Shooting the 8 Ball

After a player has pocketed all of the balls in his numerical grouping, he next shoots the 8 ball. In shooting the 8 ball, he must call his shot, designate the pocket in which he intends to hole the ball.

A player must pocket the 8 ball as he designates. If he fails to pocket the 8 ball, he must, instead (a) cause the 8 ball to contact a cushion, or, (b) cause the cue ball to contact a cushion after it strikes the 8 ball. Failure to make the ball in the designated pocket, or to complete either (a) or (b) above, causes the player to lose the game.

If a player inadvertently pockets the 8 ball before pocketing all of the balls in his numerical grouping, he loses the game.

If the player pockets the 8 ball on a combination, he loses the game.

If the 8 ball is the player's object ball, and he fails to strike the 8 ball with the cue ball, he loses the game.

If the cue ball scratches into a pocket while the player is shooting for the 8 ball, the player loses the game.

If the 8 ball scratches into a pocket other than the designated pocket, the player loses the game.

Section 5, Spotting Balls

When a player has been given an opportunity of placing the cue ball within the head string, and the object ball also rests within the head string, the object ball is to be spotted at the foot spot or on the long string. Should two or more object balls be located within the head string, the ball nearest the head string itself is to be spotted at the foot spot.

ROTATION

Section 1, Equipment

The game is played with a cue ball and fifteen object balls numbered from 1 to 15.

The balls are racked in a triangle at the foot of the table, with the 1 ball placed at the top of the triangle (facing the starting player) on the foot spot. The 2 ball is placed on the left-hand corner of the triangle; the 3 ball is placed on the right-hand corner of the triangle.

Section 2, Object of the Game

Beginning with the 1 ball, players must pocket balls in numerical order, receiving a point total on each shot equal to the numerical designations of the pocketed balls. (The 1 ball is valued at 1 point; the 6 ball at 6 points, etc.) The first player or team to score 61 points wins the game.

Section 3, Play of the Game

Contestants lag or draw lots to determine order of play.

The starting player may locate the cue ball anywhere within the head string.

On each stroke, the cue ball must make contact with the proper (lowest-numbered) object ball, before striking any other ball. When legal contact is made, player receives credit for all balls pocketed on the stroke (in the numerical designation of each of the balls). For example, if the object ball is the 3 ball, and the player strikes the 3 ball and pockets it, and then pockets the 12 ball, the player is to receive credit for 15 points. If the object ball is the 3 ball, and the player makes only the 12 ball, but the cue ball first strikes the 3 ball, the player is to receive credit for 12 points, and his inning is to continue.

Section 4, Spotting Balls

Object balls are spotted when the following occurs:

a) when the cue ball fails to strike the proper (lowest-numbered) object ball, all object balls pocketed on the stroke are to be spotted.

b) when the cue ball "scratches" into a pocket, all object balls on the stroke are to be spotted.

c) when object balls are driven from the table, they are to be returned to the table and spotted.

Balls are to be spotted along the "long string"—a line perpendicular to the foot string, and running from the foot spot to the foot rail. Should the cue ball or any object balls occupy the long string, thereby interfering with the placement of balls to be spotted, the balls to be spotted are to be placed in front of or behind the obstructing balls. The cue ball or other object balls are never to be moved from the long string to make room for balls to be spotted.

Should two or more balls be pocketed illegally on the same shot, they are to be spotted in numerical sequence.

Section 5, Scratch Shots

A player "scratches" when he pockets the cue ball. He loses his inning and balls pocketed on the stroke must be spotted. The opposing player places the cue ball within the head string.

If the cue ball is driven from the table, it is also a scratch. The player loses his inning and balls pocketed on the stroke must be spotted. The opposing player places the ball within the head string.

If a player is given the opportunity to place the ball within the head string, and the proper (lowest-numbered) object ball is also within the head string, the object ball must be placed on the foot spot or along the long string.

Failure to complete a legal stroke results in a miss and the player loses his inning.

*Billiards is new to many women,
but women are not new to the sport*